Anonymous

Short Family Prayers, with Hymns

Anonymous

Short Family Prayers, with Hymns

ISBN/EAN: 9783744779364

Printed in Europe, USA, Canada, Australia, Japan

Cover: Foto ©Lupo / pixelio.de

More available books at **www.hansebooks.com**

SHORT FAMILY PRAYERS,

WITH HYMNS.

TENTH EDITION.

NEW-YORK:
T. WHITTAKER,
No. 2 Bible House.

EXTRACT FROM THE PREFACE TO THE ENGLISH EDITION.

The writer is fully sensible that the prayers with which the reader is presented are *short*, and such, indeed, for many reasons, he designed them to be. He made it his particular study to be as concise as possible, that, let the engagements of a family be what they may, it might be impossible with such short prayers to plead a want of time for the use of them. The occasional use of the Lord's Prayer as paraphrased will be found an instructive variety.

That the children may be early taught to pray, two prayers have been added for their benefit, in language and sentiment adapted to their infant minds.

The short petitions commonly called ejaculations, because silently and suddenly darted up to Heaven, will, it is hoped, be committed to memory, and be frequently used, according as you stand in need. For, regarding ourselves as strangers and pilgrims on the earth, we should keep up a constant communion with Heaven, and be constantly lifting up our souls in prayer and praise.

NOTE TO THE PRESENT EDITION.

THIS little manual has been, and continues to be, very extensively used in England. The prayers are reprinted without alteration.

In place of the introductory matter, which is omitted, the Evangelical Knowledge Society has published a separate tract on family prayer, to which the reader is referred. The form of prayer for families, from the American Prayer-Book and a few Hymns, have been added, with the hope that they may promote the habit of singing at least a few verses in family prayer.

Ask, and it shall be given you; seek, and ye shall find; knock, and it shall be opened unto you. For every one that asketh receiveth; and he that seeketh findeth; and to him that knocketh it shall be opened. If a son shall ask bread of any of you that is a father, will he give him a stone? or if he ask a fish, will he for a fish give him a serpent? or if he shall ask an egg, will he offer him a scorpion? If ye, then, being evil, know how to give good gifts unto your children, how much more shall your heavenly Father give the Holy Spirit to them that ask him?—*Luke* 11 : 9-13.

Men ought always to pray, and not to faint.—*Luke* 18 : 1.

Watch ye therefore, and pray always.—*Luke* 21 : 36.

Praying always with all prayer and supplication in the Spirit, and watching thereunto with all perseverance.—*Ephes.* 6 : 18.

Continuing instant in prayer.—*Rom.* 12 : 12.

In every thing, by prayer and supplication, with thanksgiving, let your requests be made known unto God.—*Phil.* 4 : 6.

Continue in prayer, and watch in the same with thanksgiving.—*Col.* 4 : 2.

Pray without ceasing.—1 *Thess.* 5 : 7.

And Abraham pitched his tent, and there he builded an altar unto the Lord, and called upon the name of the Lord.—*Gen.* 12 : 8.

The sacrifices of God are a broken spirit: a broken and a contrite heart, O God, thou wilt not despise.—*Psalm* 51 : 17.

Let my prayer be set forth before thee as incense; and the lifting up of my hands as the evening sacrifice.—*Psalm* 141 : 2.

Ye are a holy priesthood, to offer up spiritual sacrifices, acceptable to God by Jesus Christ.—1 *Peter* 2 : 5.

By him therefore let us offer the sacrifice of praise to God continually —giving thanks to his Name.—*Heb.* 13 15.

FAMILY PRAYERS.

WHICH MAY BE USED AS PRIVATE PRAYERS BY SAYING
I FOR WE AND ME FOR US.

SUNDAY MORNING.

GRACIOUS God, may we ever consider it not only our duty, but our privilege, to worship thee. Grant us a grateful sense of thy mercies, and help us to praise thee for them. Give us grace to welcome this holy day with joy, and make us diligent to improve its sacred hours, to the glory of thy Name, and the salvation of our souls.

We praise thee for permitting us to behold another Sabbath. Thou hast in mercy preserved us through the night; and we beseech thee, O Lord, to bless us on this thy day with a spiritual, heavenly frame of mind! May we never neglect thy holy worship, or be lukewarm in thy blessed service; but may we always keep thy Sabbaths, and reverence thy sanctuary. May we be willing to deny ourselves any pleasure, or to suffer any loss rather than break thy commandments, which are holy, just, and good. Help us to watch over our thoughts, words, and works, remembering the Sabbath-day to keep it holy.

In public and in private, give us grace to worship thee, O God, in spirit and in truth. O Lord, pardon our sins, sanctify our hearts, and make us meet to serve thee here, and to praise thee for ever hereafter. Cheer us with the light of thy countenance, and refresh us with the dew of thy blessing.

Go with us, O Lord, we beseech thee, to thy house of prayer. Grant us grace there to confess our sins with godly sorrow; to pray in faith; and to offer up our praises with unfeigned gratitude and joy. May we come before thy presence with thanksgiving, and show ourselves glad in thee with psalms.

Look down with tender mercy on all those who, by sickness or any other adversity, may be kept from thy house of prayer. Assist them to worship thee, and cause them to rejoice that thou art every where present to hear and answer their supplications.

Bless all thy faithful ministers, and make them wise to win souls to Christ. Send forth more labourers into thy vineyard. Bless especially, those who are preaching the Gospel in heathen and distant lands. May all nations hear and receive thy holy word: and may there be added to the church, daily, numbers of such as shall be saved.

Have compassion on the Jews. Pity, O Lord, the despised outcasts of Israel. Take away their shame and their reproach. Give them faith to believe in Jesus as their anointed Prophet, Priest, and King. Gather them out of all nations whither thou hast driven them, and speedily fulfil to them that gracious promise of thy word " I will be your God, and ye shall be my people."

Cause thy holy word to come this day with power to our souls, and to the souls of our fellow-worshippers. Save and deliver us, O Lord, from vain and wandering thoughts. May we be serious and devout in thy service, and rejoice in thy favour and blessing.

And whilst we thankfully embrace every opportunity of public worship, grant that we may grow in grace and in the knowledge of our Lord and Saviour Jesus Christ; and may his love constrain us henceforth to live not unto ourselves, but unto him, who died for us, and rose again : to whom, with thee, O Father, and thee, O Holy Spirit, be ascribed all praise, now and for ever. *Amen.*

The grace of our Lord Jesus Christ, &c.

SUNDAY EVENING.

BLESSED Lord, give us grace to review with gratitude the mercies which we have this day received. Praised be thy holy Name for every Sabbath we enjoy. May the prayers we present, and the praises we offer, be always acceptable in thy sight, O Lord, our Strength and our Redeemer.

For thy Name's sake, O Lord, and for Jesus Christ's sake, be gracious and merciful unto us. All our sins are known to thee: Do thou, O Lord, forgive them. All our wants are before thee : O, do thou supply them.

Heavenly Father, thou hast been pleased to favour us beyond millions of our fallen race, and to enlighten us with the knowledge of thy word : O that we may thankfully receive thy blessings, and diligently improve them. Give us grace to live a life of faith in thee, and devotedness to thee. Let us not be Christians in word and in tongue only, but in deed and in truth.

Cherish in us, we beseech thee, whatever holy desires, or pious resolutions, thy word and Spirit may have created in us this day. Let us not be forgetful hearers, but doers of thy word. Make us watchful, that our spiritual enemy may not come and take away thy word out of our hearts, and destroy our souls. O cause it to take deep root in our hearts, and with its holy fruits to adorn our lives. Let us not be of those who hear the word with joy, and in time of temptation or persecution fall away; nor let it be choked with the cares, or the riches, or the pleasures of this life; but may we understand it and keep it, and bring forth fruit with patience.

Give us an increase of faith, hope, and love. May our faith be strong in Christ, to the honour of his name, and the salvation of our souls. May our hope be sure and steadfast. May our love, as a holy flame, purify our hearts, and shine forth in our lives.

Command thy blessing, O Lord, to rest abundantly on the labours of thy ministers. May the Gospel of our Lord Jesus Christ have free course, and be glorified. Extend his church and enlarge his kingdom. May all nations come and worship before him, and magnify his Name.

Bless, gracious Lord, our dear relations and friends, and give them the same blessings which we have asked for ourselves.

By thy great mercy defend us from all perils and dangers of this night: may we lie down in peace, and rest in safety. And when our Sabbaths are ended here on earth, may we enjoy an eternal Sabbath in heaven, and rejoice for ever in the love of Jesus Christ our Saviour. *Amen.*

The grace of our Lord Jesus Christ, &c.

MONDAY MORNING.

O THOU Father of mercies and God of all comfort, incline our hearts to love thee, and give us strength to serve thee. Make us truly humble for all our sins: and unfeignedly thankful for all thy mercies.

We have destroyed ourselves, but in thee is our help. Help us, O God of our salvation, for the glory of thy Name. O be merciful unto us, and deliver us from our sins, for thy Name's sake.

We praise thee for the safety and comfort of the past night, aud adore thee for all thy renewed mercies to us this morning. May we cheerfully renew the dedication of ourselves to thee; for thine we are, and thee we ought to serve. Give us grace to love thee truly, to serve thee faithfully, and to depend on thee without wavering.

With prayer and watchfulness may we now enter on the cares and the duties of life. Preserve us, O Lord, from the evil that is in the world. May we remember thy word, and bring forth the fruits of thy Spirit. Grant us to be pure in heart and holy in life.

Give thy blessing, O Lord, to all that thy providence may call us to do, and grant us resignation to all that thy wisdom may appoint us to suffer. May we have no will but thine, and no regard to any thing compared with thy glory.

May thy love, O blessed Jesus, reign in our hearts, and place the world under our feet. Whilst we sojourn on the earth, may we look forward to heaven as our rest, and be daily travelling towards it as our home.

We humbly beseech thee, O Father, to have mercy upon all men. Bless our Rulers whom thou hast put in authority over us. Bless the nation in which we live. Remember with thy most gracious favour, all who are near and dear to us. Cause them to know thy love, to rejoice in thy salvation, and to live after thy commandments.

Be with us, we beseech thee, through this day. Let thine arm defend and strengthen us; and let thy Holy Spirit be our guide and comforter in all our ways.

Favourably with mercy hear these our supplications and prayers, and vouchsafe to accept our praises: through Jesus Christ our only Mediator and Redeemer; to whom with Thee and the Holy Ghost, be all honour and glory, world without end.

Our Father, &c.

May grace, mercy, and peace, from God the Father, and from the Lord Jesus Christ our Saviour, and from the Holy Ghost the Comforter, be unto us, and all who belong to us, now and for ever. *Amen.*

MONDAY EVENING.

O THOU in whom we live, and move, and have our being; may we reverence thy glorious majesty, and adore thine infinite mercy. Assist us by thy grace when we come into thy presence. May we never draw near to thee, O Lord, with our mouths, or profess to honour thee with our lips, whilst our hearts are far from thee; but may we serve thee acceptably, with reverence and godly fear. Whenever we ask for spiritual blessings, may we deeply feel our need of them; and may it be the earnest desire of our souls to receive them.

We beseech thee, gracious God, to pardon all our sins. We confess our guilt: we have nothing to plead but thy promises. O be merciful unto us, for the glory of thy Name. Restore our souls, for we have sinned against thee. Heal us, O Lord, and we shall be healed; save us, and we shall be saved; for thou art our praise, and our hope is in thy mercy. May we be justified by faith, and have peace with thee, O God, through Jesus Christ our Lord.

O blessed Jesus, deliver us from the guilt and power of sin: let it have no dominion over us: but grant that we, being made free from sin, may be thy servants, have our fruit unto holiness, and our end everlasting life.

Make us careful, O Lord, to redeem our time. Keep us mindful of death and eternity; nor let us ever forget that we must soon lie down, to rise up no more in this world. When earthly comforts fail us, then grant us to rejoice the more in spiritual blessings. And when we die, may we fall asleep in Jesus, the life of them that believe, and the resurrection of the dead: may we go down to the grave full of the blessed hope of eternal life.

To thy mercy and love, O heavenly Father, we now commend ourselves. Watch over us, O thou Shepherd of Israel. Keep us by night and by day. Let thine eye be ever upon us, and thine everlasting arms round about us. Preserve us from the unholy designs of wicked men and evil spirits. Let no evil happen unto us. May our sleep be sweet and refreshing. And grant that whether we sleep or wake, live or die, we may be thine in Christ Jesus.

Bless, we beseech thee, all whom we should remember before thee; and do for us, for our dear relations and friends, for all men and our country, and for the increase of thy true religion, abundantly above all that we are able to ask or think; for Jesus Christ's sake: in whose name and words we further pray, saying,

Our Father, &c.
May grace, mercy, and peace, &c.

TUESDAY MORNING.

O LORD, our heavenly Father, Almighty and everlasting God, who hast safely brought us to the beginning of this day, what shall we render unto thee for all thy benefits conferred upon us! Adored be thy mercy for all the blessings we are continually receiving from thee. How hast thou renewed our lives and our mercies to us this morning! May all that is within us bless thy holy name. O put thy Spirit within us, and cause us to walk in thy statutes. Give us grace to glorify thee in our bodies and in our spirits, which are thine.

TUESDAY MORNING.

We praise thee, O God, for the unspeakable gift of thy dear Son, Jesus Christ our Saviour. Grant us so to believe in him, that we may have life through his Name.

We praise thee for the gift of the Holy Ghost. May our bodies be the temples of his continual abode. Let us not walk according to the course of this world, according to the spirit that worketh in the children of disobedience; but, as the children of God, may we be led by the Spirit of God, and rejoice in hope of the glory of God. Let us not resist or grieve thy Holy Spirit, but in all things obey his godly motions, to thy glory, and to our comfort and salvation. May our understanding be enlightened, our hearts sanctified, and our wills subdued, according to the working of his mighty power.

Be with us this day, to bless and uphold our souls. Grant us the joy of faith, the patience of hope, and the comfort of love; that we may rejoice in thy mercy, and give praise to thy Name. Save and deliver us from all the evils which we feel or fear, or cause them to work together for our good. Compass us about with thy favour as with a shield. Let thy loving-kindness and thy truth always preserve us.

Make us diligent, we pray thee, in the discharge of our temporal and spiritual duties. Incline us so to seek thy kingdom and righteousness, that all other things may be added unto us. Make us watchful and circumspect, ever remembering that thou, O God, seest us. In silent prayer and praise may we lift up our hearts to thee, and have frequent communion with thee. Give us grace to set an infinite value upon our souls. In the midst of life, may we think on death, judgment, and eternity; and give us all diligence to be found of Christ, in peace with God, without spot and blameless.

O Almighty Lord and everlasting God, vouchsafe, we beseech thee, to direct, sanctify, and govern, both our hearts and bodies, in the ways of thy laws, and in the works of thy commandments; that, through thy most mighty protection, both here and ever, we may be preserved in body and soul: through our Lord and Saviour Jesus Christ.

Our Father, &c.

The blessing of God Almighty, the Father, the Son, and the Holy Ghost, be upon us, and upon all whom we should remember, now and for ever. *Amen.*

TUESDAY EVENING.

O ETERNAL God, Creator and Preserver of all mankind, Giver of all spiritual grace, the Author of everlasting life, we bow down before thee this evening: and we beseech thee to accept and bless us, for the alone sake of thy dear Son Jesus Christ our Saviour. Assist us to draw near to thee, and grant us to enjoy communion with thee.

We praise thee for all thy mercies; and we beseech thee to forgive us all our sins, which are more than we can number, and greater than we can express; for in many things we offend, and that continually. Grant us daily repentance toward thee, O God, and faith toward our Lord Jesus Christ. Remember, O Lord, thy tender mercies and thy lovingkindnesses, for they have been ever of old. Remember not the sins of our youth, nor our transgressions; but according to thy mercy remember thou us, for thy goodness' sake, O Lord. Heal all our backslidings, receive us gracious y, and love us freely.

Give us grace to renounce the world; make

as willing to crucify the flesh; and strengthen us to resist the devil. Help us to deny ourselves, to take up our cross, and to follow Christ. Preserve us from every thing that would dishonour his holy Name. May we depart from all iniquity, and avoid every temptation to sin. Give us to see the evil of sin in the death of Christ, and fill us with holy zeal and indignation against it. Create in us clean hearts, O God, and renew right spirits within us. Make us more humble, more thankful, more holy.

We beseech thee, O Lord, to bless our Rulers and to endue their counsel with Thy wisdom. We pray thee also to be gracious and favourable to our country. O may it ever abound with that righteousness which exalteth a nation.

Bless the ministers of thy glorious Gospel and enable them rightly to divide the word of truth. Give them grace to warn the unruly, to comfort the feeble-minded, to support the weak, and to be patient toward all men.

Bless, Lord, all our dear relations and friends. Extend to them, we beseech thee, thy grace and favour. Give them, for Christ's sake, every blessing needful to their salvation.

TUESDAY EVENING.

Have mercy upon all men. Comfort the sick. Succour the tempted. Relieve the oppressed. Be the Father of the fatherless, and the God of the widow. Give joy to those who mourn for sin. Bind up the broken-hearted, and save such as be of a contrite spirit; giving them everlasting consolation and good hope, through thy grace and mercy in Christ Jesus.

Into thy hands we now commend ourselves, our souls and bodies. Enable us, O Lord, to bless and praise thee for all that we have received from thee: and while we rely upon thy mercy, may we ever seek thy honour and glory: through our only Mediator and Advocate, Jesus Christ our Lord.

Our Father, &c.

The blessing of God Almighty, the Father, the Son, and the Holy Ghost, be upon us and upon all whom we should remember, now and for ever. *Amen.*

WEDNESDAY MORNING.

GRACIOUS God, thou hast spared us to see the light of another day. May we approach thy throne, rejoicing in thee, and ascribing all our salvation to thee.

We thank thee, O Lord, for all thy mercies renewed to us this morning. May they increase in us a renewed sense of thy love to our souls. Draw out our desires after thee, and fix our affections upon thee. May we begin this day in thy strength, pass through it in thy fear and love, and end it to thy glory.

We praise thee for thy holy word, which thou hast given to be a lamp unto our feet, and a light unto our paths. May we walk as children of the light; and may our cheerful obedience to thy will, prove to ourselves and others that we partake of thy grace.

We bless thee, O Lord, for such a fountain of wisdom and holiness; and we pray, that in all our troubles we may hope in thy word, and derive all our comfort from it. May it remove our doubts and calm our fears, and show us the way wherein we should go.

When our souls cleave to the dust, may we be upheld by its quickening and sanctifying power. May it dwell in us richly, in all wisdom and spiritual understanding. May we love its precepts, fear its threatenings, and believe its promises, to the saving of our souls.

Incline us to search the Scriptures daily. May we not only read, but also mark, learn, and inwardly digest them; and know, to our peace and joy, that blessed Jesus of whom they testify. Grant that we may have frequent occasions to rejoice, and to say of thy words, They are spirit and they are life.

We pray thee, O Lord, to send forth thy light and thy truth to the nations that are sitting in darkness, and in the shadow of death. Bless all the societies established in this land for the making known the revelation of thy will. Make them the glory of our land, and the joy of the whole earth. Give to all who are engaged in these labours wisdom, zeal, humility, and love.

And as we pray for the spread of thy word at home and abroad, so we beseech thee also to nspire continually the universal church with the spirit of truth, unity and concord: and grant that all they that do confess thy holy Name, may agree in the truth of thy holy word, and live in unity and godly love.

And now, O Lord, while we offer up our morning sacrifice of praise for all thy mercies, we beseech thee to forgive us all our sins, and to bless, preserve, and keep us this day, through Jesus Christ our Saviour.

Our Father, &c. The grace, &c.

WEDNESDAY EVENING.

O THOU that hearest prayer, pour down upon us the Spirit of grace and of supplication. Teach us how to pray. Help us to make known our wants unto thee, who alone canst supply them. Enable us so to ask, that we may receive, and so to seek that we may find. May we pray in the Spirit, and be accepted of thee, O heavenly Father, through thy beloved Son Jesus Christ onr Saviour. Through him may we obtain mercy, and find grace to help in every time of need.

May we always approach thee in humility and sincerity; for the prayer of the upright is thy delight. Let us not regard iniquity in our hearts; for if we do, thou wilt not hear us.

May we pray in faith, and never doubt thy power or will to save all who come to thee by Jesus Christ. O help us to come to thee in his Name, and to plead the atonement of his precious blood. In all our prayers may we rely on his gracious mediation, and trust in his all-prevailing intercession.

May we pray without fainting, and have strength to pursue our heavenly course without weariness. Grant us to be more frequent and more earnest in our prayers; and be thou graciously pleased to answer them, O Lord, according to the multitude of thy tender mercies.

Pardon our sins; and daily renew us, we beseech thee, after the image of Christ Jesus our Lord. Sanctify our hearts, and satisfy our souls with thy mercy.

But whilst we pray for ourselves, let us never be unmindful of others. Look down O Lord, on our dear relations and friends, and visit them with thy salvation. May it be their privilege to know thee, and their blessedness to rejoice in thee.

Comfort and succour all them who in

this transitory life are in trouble, sorrow, need, sickness, or any other adversity.

Bless our Rulers and our country. Pour out upon us the spirit of repentance and reformation. Grant us to be a people fearing thee and working righteousness.

Send forth the riches of thy grace, and make known to all nations the saving power of thy word, Let all the ends of the earth see the salvation of our God, and rejoice in Jesus our exalted Prince and Saviour.

Finally, Lord, we bless thee for all thy goodness to us; and we beseech thee still to preserve and keep us from all evil. By night and by day may we be under the continual protection of thy good providence. Extend thy love to us, and thy care over us this night; and give us grace to pray to thee without ceasing, till we are called to praise thee for ever in heaven; through Jesus Christ, our blessed Lord and Saviour. *Amen.*

Our Father, &c. The grace, &c.

THURSDAY MORNING.

GLORIOUS Jehovah, give us such a sense of thy majesty and of thy mercy, as shall fill us with deep humility. Thou art holy, but we are unholy by nature and by practice. Lord, have mercy upon us; and for Christ's sake pardon our sins, and make clean our hearts within us. Give us grace to watch against the first motions of sin in the heart, and strengthen us to suppress and overcome them.

Assist us by thy grace to watch over our thoughts, words, and works. May we hate vain thoughts, and daily become more spiritual and heavenly-minded. Help us to keep our tongues as it were with a bridle. May we be slow to speak, slow to wrath. Save us, O Lord, from a contentious spirit, and grant that we may speak evil of no man. Suffer us not by word or deed to grieve thy blessed Spirit, or dishonour our Christian name. Grant us to live in the daily exercise of that pure and peaceable wisdom, which cometh down from above. May we show forth our wisdom in refraining our lips from every evil word, and our feet from every evil way. Let us carefully watch the principle, and mark the end of our actions. May love to Christ be the principle, and his glory the end, of all that we do.

Help us, O God of our salvation, to mortify and subdue the pride and wickedness of our hearts. Deliver us from self-seeking and self-pleasing. Grant that we may be humble in prosperity, and patient in adversity. Make us willing to be last of all, or the servants of all if so thou in all things mayest be glorified.

We beseech thee, O Lord, to bless and defend our Rulers and our country. Continue to us the pure light of thy holy Gospel. Let there be peace and truth in our day: yea, let truth and justice, religion and piety, be established among us for all generations. Bless all ranks and degrees of men. Make the poor rich in faith, and the rich poor in spirit. Bless and prosper abundantly the ministers of thy holy word. Bless them in their own souls, and grant them to be a blessing to the souls of others. Send forth the messengers of thy grace to all nations and fill the earth with the knowledge and love of Christ our Saviour.

We praise thee, O Lord, for thy preserving

care, which hath been over us to the present moment. We bless thee for the mercies of the past night, and for thy goodness to us this morning. Give us grace to begin and end every day with prayer and praise; and, vile as we are, and unworthy of the least of all thy mercies, O do thou bless us, and accept us in Jesus Christ, our only Mediator and Redeemer; who hath taught us to pray, saying, Our Father, &c.

God the Father, God the Son, God the Holy Ghost, bless, preserve, and keep us: the Lord mercifully with his favour look upon us, and so fill us with all spiritual benediction and grace, that we may so live in this life, that in the world to come we may have life everlasting. *Amen.*

THURSDAY EVENING.

WE praise thee, O Lord, for all thy mercies to us this day. Thou daily pourest out thy benefits upon us. Blessed be thy Name, O thou God of our salvation. May we derive all our joy and peace from thee, and find all our comfort and happiness in living for thee. Establish, we pray thee, that kingdom within us which is righteousness, and peace, and joy in the Holy Ghost. In this dying world may our faith be in Christ, the Resurrection and the life. In this changing world, may we never be moved away from the blessed hope of the Gospel. Let not our faith be overthrown; let not our hope sink in despair; let not our love fail but may they be firmly fixed on Jesus Christ, the same yesterday, to-day, and for ever.

Lead us in the narrow path of eternal life, and uphold our goings, that our footsteps slip not. Enable us so to pass through this world of sin and danger, that we may at last reach the heavenly Canaan. O bring us to that rest which remaineth for the people of God. Whilst we live may we live unto thee, O Lord; and when we die may we die unto thee.

Bless us, O Lord, as a family. Forgive us all our sins, and subdue in us every unholy temper and disposition. May we so dwell in love, that thou, the God of love and peace, mayest be with us. Bless our dear friends. Forgive our enemies, and turn their hearts and give us grace freely to forgive them, even as we hope to be forgiven. Let the same mind be in us which was also in Christ Jesus. Give us grace so to learn of Him, who was meek and lowly in heart, that we may find rest to our souls.

Be gracious and favourable, O Lord, to our country. Let thy providence be our defence, and thy presence our glory. Give to all who are in authority wisdom and courage to use it to the honour of thy Name, and the welfare of those whom thou hast put in subjection under them. Grant to all who are in places of public trust, grace to be faithful to the public interest.

Bless and prosper thy holy church universal, and especially that part of it to which we belong. Increase the number of thy faithful people, and make them fruitful in every good word and work.

Keep us mindful, O Lord, that the end of all things is at hand. Let us not be weary in well-doing, but may we be sober, and watch unto prayer.

May we lie down this night reposing our souls and bodies upon thy mercy and love, O God our Saviour. And when our day of grace is ended, then as faithful servants may we enter into the joy of our Lord, and rejoice in the glory of our blessed and exalted Redeemer: to whom, with the Father and the Holy Spirit, be ascribed everlasting praise. *Amen.*

Our Father, &c.
God the Father, God the Son, &c.

FRIDAY MORNING.

O THOU ever-blessed and glorious **Jehovah**, we are unworthy to come into thy presence; we are unworthy to call upon thy Name; we deserve nothing but thy wrath. But with thee, O Lord, there is mercy, and with thee is plenteous redemption. Save, Lord, or we perish. Oh cast us not away from thy presence. Incline thine ear, and hear us. Grant unto us pardon and peace, that we may serve thee with a quiet mind.

Teach us thy ways, O Lord, and enable us to **walk** in thy truth. Give us grace to delight in thy law, which is holy, just and good. May we be followers of thee, O God, as dear children; and walk in love, as Christ also loved us, and gave himself for us. Prepare us for the duties and trials for which we may be called, for we know not what a day may bring forth. Let thy wisdom guide us, and thy power uphold and strengthen us.

Give us not up to the sinful desires of our hearts, neither leave us to follow our vain imaginations. Suffer not the enemies of our peace and salvation to prevail against us. But grant that we, walking in thy fear, and in the comfort of the Holy Ghost, may enjoy that peace which passeth understanding, and which the world can neither give nor take away.

Living in a world of sin and sorrow, we bless thee, O Lord, for all thy servants departed this life in thy faith and fear. Give us grace to follow them, who through faith and patience now inherit the promises. Help us to fight the good fight of faith, that we may lay hold on eternal life.

Regard with thy favour and blessing our dear relations and friends. May they all partake of thy grace here, and of everlasting glory hereafter.

Be merciful to thy church and people, and grant that, however dispersed or distressed, they may all be united and comforted together in Christ. Supply the wants of all who believe in his Name, and are devoted to his service. In all times of their tribulation, good Lord, deliver them.

Bless the ministers of the Gospel—all who preach Jesus Christ as the way, the truth, and the life. Add to their number, and increase their faithfulness and zeal. May they speak the truth in love; and give themselves continually to prayer, and to the ministry of the word.

Bless, gracious God, our country, and all whom thy providence hath set over us; and may it be our holy determination to serve thee, O Lord, and to obey every ordinance of man for thy sake.

Accept our praises, O Lord, for every blessing we enjoy. May thy mercies draw our hearts towards thee in gratitude, and unite them to thee in love. Finally, we beseech thee to bless us when we lie down and when we rise up, and to bless us in our going out and coming in, from this time forth for evermore: through Jesus Christ our Saviour; in whose holy name and words we farther pray, saying,

Our Father, &c

[Blessing on next page]

The Lord bless us and keep us; the Lord make his face to shine upon us. and be gracious unto us; the Lord lift up his countenance upon us, and give us peace, both now and evermore. *Amen.*

FRIDAY EVENING.

O LORD God of our salvation, from whom alone all good things do come, we beseech thee to supply all our wants out of thy fulness, and of thy tender mercy to pardon all our sins. Our sins are many and great: O Lord, forgive them. Our mercies are innumerable and undeserved: O make us truly thankful for them.

We live upon thy bountiful grace and mercy: enable us, we beseech thee, to live to thy honour and glory. May the love of thee take full possession of our hearts, and be manifested in our lives. Give us grace to walk before thee in holiness and righteousness all our days.

May we serve thee with a perfect heart, and with a willing mind. Laying aside every weight with the sin that doth most easily beset us, may we run with patience the race that is set before us, looking unto Jesus, the Author and Finisher of our faith.

O God our Saviour, thou that givest strength unto thy people, let us not faint or be weary in our minds; but do thou comfort and support us, that we may steadfastly endure unto the end. Whilst some are departing from thee, give us grace to cleave to thee with full purpose of heart; that, being faithful unto death, we may receive the crown of glory which fadeth not away.

Save us, O God, from those covetous desires which pierce the soul with many sorrows; and from that love of the world by which so many are enslaved to its pleasures. Turn away our eyes from beholding vanity, and quicken thou us in thy way. Grant us to be spiritually minded, which is life and peace.

Incline us to seek the glory of His Name, whose tender mercy sought the salvation of our souls: and may the care of our souls be the chief concern of our lives. Oh that each of us may say in truth, of thy beloved Son, He is my beloved Saviour. May it be manifest to us, that we are accepted of God the Father, and redeemed of God the Son, by being sanctified of God the Holy Ghost.

Let the close of this and every day remind us that all things are coming to an end. As good servants of Christ, our blessed Lord and Master, may we be always looking for his coming. Grant that it may be our blessedness to be found watching, and our reward to enter into the joy of our Lord. Save us in the hour of death; and in the day of judgment, good Lord, deliver us.

Give thy blessing, O Lord. to our Rulers, and let it rest abundantly on our country. Be gracious to our dear relations and friends, and make them to be numbered with thy saints in glory everlasting.

To thy fatherly care we now commend ourselves. May we always abide under the shadow of thy wings, and know to our peace and joy, the God in whom we believe. And should we arise in the morning, to enter again on the duties of this life, may thy fear and love dwell in our hearts, and influence all our doings. May thy grace and mercy preserve us from every evil way, and enable us so to pass through things temporal, that we finally lose not the things eternal.

We ask all in thy name, and for thy sake, O blessed Jesus, who art ever worthy, with the Father and the Holy Spirit, to receive equal honour and endless praise; and who hast graciously taught us to pray, saying,

Our Father, &c.

The Lord bless us and keep us, &c.

SATURDAY MORNING.

BLESSED Lord, thy mercies are new every morning. O help us to praise thee for thy faithfulness and truth.

Preserved by thy goodness and mercy to the beginning of this day, we bless thee for thy care of us during the night. We praise thee for all thy mercies, temporal and spiritual, known and unknown. Gracious God, we are inclined to forget thee, and prone to depart from thee. Henceforth enable us to set thee always before us; and whether we eat or drink, or whatsoever we do, to do all to thy glory.

We beseech thee, O Lord, to pardon all our sins: cleanse us from their guilt, and deliver us from their power. Show unto us more of the vanity of the world, the evil of sin, the worth of our souls, the glory of Christ, and the beauty of holiness.

May thy blessed word be our rule, and thy Holy Spirit our Guardian and Guide, in all our ways. Let us never follow the multitude to do evi . May we frequently and seriously inquire what are we doing, and whither are we going? Make us careful to abstain from all appearance of evil, that the ways of truth and holiness may not, on our account, be spoken against. O may it be our study to adorn the doctrine of God our Saviour in all things.

May we be zealous for the honour and glory of his Name. Let us never feel cold or indifferent to the cause of Christ and his Gospel; but may our hearts burn within us to spread abroad the knowledge of His love, who died that we might live, and who now ever liveth to make intercession for us.

O let the earth be filled with the knowledge of our Lord and Saviour Jesus Christ. Blessed Jesus, seek and save the lost sheep of the house of Israel, and bring the fulness of the Gentiles into thy fold. Lead into the way of truth those who are wandering from it ; and keep thy people, O Lord, steadfast in the faith, and hope, and love of the Gospel; and that they may persevere unto the end, grant them grace to take heed lest they fall.

Bless and assist thy ministers this day in meditating on thy word. To-morrow may they all go forth in thy strength, and turn many to righteousness.

We beseech thee, heavenly Father, to hear the prayers of thy children, and to give thy Holy Spirit to them that ask thee. Let those that seek thee be joyful and glad in thee; and let such as love thy salvation say continually, The Lord be magnified, who hath pleasure in the prosperity of his servants.

Bless us, O Lord, we beseech thee, together with our dear relations and friends. Convict, convert, and save them forever. Bless us, and we shall be blessed indeed. Bless us and them with the knowledge of ourselves as sinners, and of Christ Jesus as our Lord and Saviour: to whom be glory, now and for ever. *Amen.*

Our Father, &c.

May grace, mercy, and peace, from God the Father, and from the Lord Jesus Christ our Saviour, and from the Holy Ghost the Comforter, be unto us, and all who belong to us, now and for ever. *Amen.*

SATURDAY EVENING.

O THOU gracious and merciful God blessed be thy Name for preserving us in a world of sin and danger. We praise thee for having brought us in safety not only to the end of another day, but also of another week.

We bless thee, O Lord, for all the mercies which we have received from thee; and we pray and beseech thee for Christ's sake to pardon all the sins which we have committed against thee. O blot them out of the book of thy remembrance; let them not appear in judgment against us, but cleanse us from their guilt in the precious blood of Christ our Saviour.

Create and cherish in our souls a hungering and thirsting after righteousness. By faith, with thanksgiving, may we daily feed upon the true Bread which came down from heaven. May the Holy Spirit be in us as a well of water, springing up unto everlasting life, in holy desires and heavenly affections. Grant, Lord, that we may never thirst after the riches or the pleasures of the world neither

SATURDAY EVENING.

let us be overcharged with its cares, lest that day of Christ's appearing to judge the world come upon us when we look not for it.

Keep us in safety, we beseech thee, this night; and should we see the light of another Lord's Day help us, O Lord, to deny ourselves all unnecessary sleep and self-indulgence. Give us grace and strength to rise up early in the morning. Early in the morning may we direct our prayers and praises unto thee, and look up to the throne of thy grace in humble expectation of thy mercy. May we redeem from our beds some portion of time for prayer and praise, that our souls may prosper and be in health.

Prepare us for the sacred duties of the Holy Day, Visit our souls when we awake, with the light of thy heavenly grace. May we arise strengthened and refreshed for thy service. Draw out our desires after thee, and raise our affections to thee. In private devotion, in family prayer, and in public worship, may we enjoy communion with thee, O God, and know thy love to our souls, who art gracious and full of compassion.

Bless thy ministers, and crown their labours with success. Give them wisdom as well as zeal. Fill them with love, and clothe them with humility.

Bless and defend thy Church. Stir up thy faithful people, O Lord, to pray for her peace, and to labour for her prosperity. May all who name the Name of Christ depart from iniquity. Give to those who profess to abide in him, grace to walk even as he walked. May our whole life be a life of faith in and obedience to Christ, the Son of God.

And now, gracious Lord, for all thy patience with us, thy care over us, and thy continual mercies to us, blessed be thy holy Name for ever and ever: through Jesus Christ, our only Mediator and Redeemer.

Our Father, &c.

May grace, mercy and peace, from God the Father, and from the Lord Jesus Christ our Saviour, and from the Holy Ghost the Comforter, be unto us, and all who belong to us, now and for ever. *Amen.*

PRAYERS

TO BE USED IN FAMILIES AS AN OCCASIONAL SUBSTITUTE OR ADDITION IN WHOLE OR IN PART TO ANY OF THE PRECEDING.

MORNING PRAYER.

ALMIGHTY and everlasting God, in whom we live and move and have our being; we, thy needy creatures, render thee our humble praises, for thy preservation of us from the beginning of our lives to this day, and especially for having delivered us from the dangers of the past night. To thy watchful providence we owe it,* (that no disturbance hath come nigh us or our dwelling: but, that we are brought in safety to the beginning of this day.) For these thy mercies we bless and magnify thy glorious name; humbly beseeching thee to accept this our morning sacrifice of praise and thanksgiving; for his sake who lay down in the grave, and rose again for us, thy Son, our Saviour Jesus Christ. *Amen.*

Acknowledgment of God's mercy and preservation especially through the night past.

* *When disturbances of any kind befall a family, instead of this, say, that notwithstanding our dangers, we are brought in safety to the beginning of this day.*

Dedication of soul and body to God's service, with a resolution, to be growing daily in goodness.

AND, since it is of thy mercy, O, gracious Father, that another day is added to our lives; we here dedicate both our souls and our bodies to thee and thy service, in a sober, righteous, and godly life: in which resolution, do thou, O merciful God, confirm and strengthen us; that, as we grow in age, we may grow in grace, and in the knowledge of our Lord and Saviour Jesus Christ. *Amen.*

Prayer for grace to enable us to perform that resolution.

BUT O God, who knowest the weakness and corruption of our nature, and the manifold temptations which we daily meet with; we humbly beseech thee to have compassion on our infirmities, and to give us the constant assistance of thy Holy Spirit; that we may be effectually restrained from sin, and excited to our duty. Imprint upon our hearts such a dread of thy judgments, and such a grateful sense of thy goodness to us, as may make us both afraid and ashamed to offend thee. And, above all, keep in our mind a lively remembrance of that great day, in which we must give a strict account of our thoughts, words, and actions; and according to the works done in the body, be eternally rewarded or punished, by him whom thou hast appointed the Judge of quick and dead, thy Son Jesus Christ our Lord. *Amen.*

IN particular, we implore thy grace and protection for the ensuing day. Keep us temperate in our meats and drinks, and diligent in our several callings. Grant us patience under any afflictions, thou shalt see fit to lay on us, and minds always contented with our present condition. Give us grace to be just and upright in all our dealings; quiet and peaceable; full of compassion; and ready to do good to all men, according to our abilities and opportunities. Direct us in all our ways *(and prosper the works of our hands in the business of our several stations.) Defend us from all dangers and adversities; and be graciously pleased to take us, and all things belonging to us under thy fatherly care and protection. These things, and whatever else thou shalt see necessary and convenient to us, we

For grace to guide and keep us the following day, and for God's blessing on the business of the same.

* *On Sunday morning, instead of this, say, and let thy Holy Spirit accompany us to the place of thy public worship, making us serious and attentive, and raising our minds from the thoughts of this world to the consideration of the next, that we may fervently join in the prayers and praises of thy Church, and listen to our duty with honest hearts, in order to practise it.*

humbly beg, through the merits and mediation of thy Son Jesus Christ our Lord and Saviour. *Amen.*

THE grace of our Lord Jesus Christ, and the love of God, and the fellowship of the Holy Ghost, be with us all evermore. *Amen.*

———◆———

EVENING PRAYER.

MOST merciful God, who art of purer eyes than to behold iniquity and hast promised forgiveness to all those who confess and forsake their sins; we come before thee in an humble sense of our own unworthiness, acknowledging the manifold transgressions of thy righteous laws which we would now recall in thy presence.* But, O gracious Father, who desirest not the death of a sinner, look upon us, we beseech thee, in mercy, and forgive us all our transgressions. Make us deeply sensible of the great evil of them; and work in us an hearty contrition; that we may

Confession of sins, with a prayer for contrition and pardon.

* *Here let him who reads make a short pause, that every one may secretly confess the sins and failings of that day.*

EVENING PRAYER.

obtain forgiveness at thy hands, who art ever ready to receive humble and penitent sinners; for the sake of thy Son Jesus Christ, our only Saviour and Redeemer. *Amen.*

AND lest, through our own frailty, or the temptations which encompass us, we be drawn again into sin, vouchsafe us, we beseech thee, the direction and assistance of thy Holy Spirit. Reform whatever is amiss in the temper and disposition of our souls; that no unclean thoughts, unlawful designs, or inordinate desires, may rest there. Purge our hearts from envy, hatred, and malice: that we may never suffer the sun to go down upon our wrath; but may always go to our rest in peace, charity, and good-will, with a conscience void of offence towards thee, and towards men: That so, we may be preserved pure and blameless, unto the coming of our Lord and Saviour Jesus Christ. *Amen.* *Prayer for grace to reform and grow better.*

AND accept, O Lord, our intercessions for all mankind. Let the light of thy Gospel shine upon all nations, and may as many as have received it, live as becomes it. Be gracious unto thy Church; and grant that every member of the same, in *The Intercession.*

his vocation and ministry, may serve thee faithfully. Bless all in authority over us; and so rule their hearts and strengthen their hands, that they may punish wickedness and vice, and maintain thy true religion and virtue. Send down thy blessings, temporal and spiritual, upon all our relations, friends, and neighbours. Reward all who have done us good, and pardon all those who have done or wish us evil, and give them repentance and better minds. Be merciful to all who are in any trouble; and do thou, the God of pity, administer to them according to their several necessities, for his sake who went about doing good, thy Son our Saviour Jesus Christ. *Amen.*

The Thanksgiving. TO our prayers, O Lord, we join our unfeigned thanks for all thy mercies; for our being, our reason, and all other endowments and faculties of soul and body; for our health, friends, food and raiment, and all the other comforts and conveniences of life. Above all, we adore thy mercy in sending thy only Son into the world, to redeem us from sin and eternal death, and in giving us the knowledge and sense of our duty towards thee. We bless thee for thy patience with us, notwithstanding our many and great

EVENING PRAYER. 51

provocations; for all the directions, assistances, and comforts of thy Holy Spirit; for thy continual care and watchful providence over us through the whole course of our lives; and particularly for the mercies and benefits of the past day: beseeching thee to continue these thy blessings to us; and to give us grace to show our thankfulness in a sincere obedience to his laws, through whose merits and intercession we received them all, thy Son our Saviour Jesus Christ. *Amen.*

IN particular, we beseech thee to continue thy gracious protection to us this night. Defend us from all dangers and mischiefs and from the fear of them; that we may enjoy such refreshing sleep as may fit us for the duties of the following day. Make us ever mindful of the time when we shall lie down in the dust; and grant us grace always to live in such a state, that we may never be afraid to die: so that, living and dying, we may be thine, through the merits and satisfaction of thy Son Christ Jesus, in whose name we offer up these our imperfect prayers. *Amen.* *[Prayer for God's protection through the night following]*

The grace of our Lord Jesus Christ, &c

OCCASIONAL PRAYERS.

A PRAYER BEFORE RECEIVING THE LORD'S SUPPER.

GRACIOUS Lord, I am now invited to thy table; may I go to it with a broken and a contrite heart. O blessed Jesus, may I look upon thee, whom my sins have pierced, and mourn. Grant to me pardon and peace, through the atonement of thy precious blood. Cleanse me from my sins, and clothe me with thy righteousness. And while I feel my guilt as a sinner, grant me, O thou crucified Saviour, to rejoice in thy mercy. Increase my faith in thee, and fill my soul with love to thee.

Let the bread, which I hope to receive, remind me of thy body, which was broken for our sins, and bruised for our iniquities; and may I feed on thee in my heart by faith, with thanksgiving. May the wine bring to my remembrance thy precious blood, which cleanseth from all sin, and which was shed to make reconciliation for iniquity. May I receive it with thankfulness, and be filled with all joy and peace in believing, and abound in hope, through the power of the Holy Ghost. May I taking the bread and the wine, show my utter dependence for salvation upon that death upon the cross which they represent to my soul. May I do all in remembrance of thee, O Lord Jesus, and in obedience to thy word. O thou Lamb of God, that madest peace by the blood of thy cross, speak peace to my soul; and be thou graciously pleased to manifest thyself unto me as thou dost not unto the world.

May I return from thy table, O Lord, strengthened and refreshed for thy holy and blessed service. Didst thou die for me? oh let me live to thee. Give me grace to deny myself, to take up my cross, and to follow thee. Bought with a price which angels cannot reckon, may I glorify thee both in my body and in my spirit, which are thine. Help me to crucify the flesh, with its affections and lusts. Grant me to be more meek and lowly in heart, and to be more spiritually minded, which is life and peace.

Behold the sorrows of those who are filled with groundless fears lest they should eat and drink unworthily. Enable them to cast themselves upon Christ, and so discern the Lord's body. Comfort those whom Satan would drive to despair; and give rest to all who are weary and heavy laden with sin. Convince of their guilt and misery those who will not come to the feast which thou hast prepared; and have mercy upon those who may presume to come without that preparation of heart which is from thee, and consists in entire surrender of soul and body to thee. Show them their danger, whether they are madly living in sin, or vainly trusting in their own righteousness.

O thou divine Saviour, who knowest what is in man, help me to judge, and try, and examine myself, whether I be in the faith. And when the tares shall no longer grow together with the wheat, then may thy holy angels gather me, with all thy redeemed, into thy kingdom, to rejoice in thy love, and to praise thy Name, for ever and ever. *Amen.*

HYMN.

' *He brought me to the banquetting house, and his banner over me was love.*' CANT. ii. 4.

1. LOWLY as Sharon's rose, and fair
 As lilies which the valleys bear,
 My soul would be, to meet my Lord,
 Belov'd and honour'd and ador'd.

2 He leads me in the safe retreat,
 Defended from the burning heat:
 Whene'er I fainted, o'er my head
 The banner of his love he spread.

3 With living bread and sacred wine
He cheers this sinking heart of mine;
Confirms anew his covenant grace,
And fills me with abounding peace.

4. Oh never may that peace depart,
But dwell in me, and keep my heart!
From thee I never would remove,
Nor grieve thee, nor offend thy love

A PRAYER AFTER RECEIVING THE LORD'S SUPPER.

HELP me, O blessed Jesus, to meditate on thy love. Let it inspire my heart and influence my life. Give me grace now to renew that surrender of myself to thee, which I made at thy table, and in the presence of thy people. Let thy love in dying for me constrain me to live more and more to thy glory. May I feel those infinite obligations by which I am bound to love and serve thee. Redeemed, not with corruptible things, as silver and gold, but with thy precious blood, oh may I keep back nothing from thee, but devote myself, and all that I have, unto thee. Help me to give thee my heart; and do thou sanctify and cleanse it, to the glory of thy Name.

O merciful Saviour, I praise thee for thy dying love, which has been brought to my remembrance this day. If any godly sorrow, if any lively faith, were excited, not unto me, O Lord, not unto me, but unto thy Name, be all the glory. Cherish every holy desire and purpose of heart to do thy will, O God: let them not be as the morning cloud or the early dew which passeth away; but confirm and strengthen that which thou hast wrought in me. Graft in my heart the love of thy Name; increase in me true religion; nourish me with all goodness; and of thy great mercy keep me in the same.

And forasmuch as without thee I am not able to please thee, mercifully grant that thy Holy Spirit may in all things direct and rule my heart. May I hold such communion with thee, my Saviour and my God, as may increase me in my love and likeness to thee. Grant that I may daily become more meet for that blessed world, where I shall no more desire such pledges of thy love, or want such memorials of thy grace, but shall see thee face to face, and be filled with everlasting wonder, love, and praise.

May all who have waited upon thee this

day, find their spiritual strength renewed. Comfort and succour those who may be called in any way to suffer for thy truth. May they steadfastly look up to heaven, and by faith behold the glory that shall be revealed.

And now, Lord, what wait I for? truly my hope is in thee. O fill me with thy grace and heavenly benediction, for sweet is thy mercy. And when thou shalt come to be glorified in thy saints, and to be admired in all them that believe, then may I sit down with Abraham, and Isaac, and Jacob, at thy marriage supper, O thou Son of God, and love and adore thee who art the Lamb, for ever and ever. *Amen*

A PRAYER

FOR THE

INCREASE AND PROSPERITY OF CHRIST'S CHURCH AND KINGDOM.

WE humbly beseech thee, O heavenly Father, to bless and prosper the word of thy grace. Send forth thy light and thy truth to all nations. Hasten the fulfilment of all that thou hast promised concerning the glory of thy dear Son, and extend his kingdom over all the earth. Let him be the Light of the Gentiles, and the Glory of thy people Israel. Lord, we plead with thee for the sake of thy great Name, the truth of thy promises, and the happiness of thy creatures; and beseech thee to give unto thy Son the Heathen for his inheritance, and the uttermost parts of the earth for his possession. Arise, O God, and plead thine own cause. Have respect unto the covenant of grace and mercy, for the dark places of the earth are full of the habitations of cruelty. How long shall the prince of darkness usurp the promised inheritance of thy beloved Son Jesus Christ our Saviour. O let the throne of the Redeemer be established on the ruins of Satan's kingdom. Pull down the strong-holds of Antichrist; and convert all nations, making them obedient to the faith of the Gospel.

And while we thus pray, we also bless thee, O Lord, for the general desire thou hast created to spread the word of thy truth and righteousness throughout the world. Lord, increase it, we beseech thee, a hundred fold. Give thy blessing to all the Societies, in this and in other nations, which have for their object thy glory and the salvation of man. Guide the minds of those who conduct their affairs. In all their trials and difficulties comfort and support them.

Regard, we beseech thee, with thy most gracious favour, all the Ministers of thy Gospel, and especially those who are preaching to the poor Heathen the unsearchable riches of Christ. Water both them and their labours with the continual dew of thy heavenly blessing. Send forth the messengers of thy grace with the good tidings of salvation; and prepare thy way before them. May every valley be exalted, and every hill made low; may the crooked ways be made straight, and the rough places plain; that thy word in all nations may have free course and be glorified.

May all Christian Missionaries be chosen vessels to bear thy name unto the Heathen. Bless them with health of body and peace of mind. Preserve them pure in doctrine and holy in life. Grant that they may never lose that first love which constrained them for thy Name's sake to leave their country, and all that was near and dear unto them. Give them grace to be faithful unto death that they may receive the crown of life. May thy Gospel be so preached by them, that it may drop as the rain, and distil as the dew: may it come down as rain upon the mown grass, as showers that water the earth. May the wilderness be glad, and the desert rejoice and blossom as the rose; may it blossom abundantly, and rejoice even with joy and singing. Let thy word never return unto thee void but prosper, and accomplish thy purposes of grace and mercy to a lost and ruined world. May all nations see the glory of the Lord, and the excellency of our God, and be filled with holiness, peace, and love

Look down. O Lord, with tender compassion

on thine ancient people the Jews, and receive them again to the arms of thy mercy. O pity the seed of Abraham thy servant, and the children of Jacob thy chosen. Look not to their stubbornness, nor to their iniquity, nor to their sin; but remember Abraham, and Isaac, and Jacob, thy servants; and hasten in these latter days the fulfilment of all the glory thou hast promised to Israel thy people. Take away the veil from off their hearts: grant them to know that Jesus Christ is their true Messiah, and that he came to visit and redeem his people. Save them from that unbelief and hardness of heart which have brought such guilt and misery upon them; and give them faith so to believe in Jesus, that they may say, " Surely he hath borne *our* griefs and carried *our* sorrows: *We* did esteem him smitten of God and afflicted; but he was wounded for *our* transgressions, he was bruised for *our* iniquities, and by his stripes *we* are healed." O let them not abide in unbelief, but bring them into thy church, O Lord God of Israel, to the glory of thy Name, who only doest wondrous things.

We beseech thee to pour out thy Spirit, to give light and life to all who are dead in sin. It is not by any human wisdom or power that the nations of the earth can be converted unto **thee**; but by thy Spirit, O Lord. Stir up thy faithful people to pray for the gift of the Holy Ghost, in all his mighty power; and do thou hear and answer their supplications. Send down from above a more abundant measure of his Divine influence, to carry on the great work of salvation; that the blessed Redeemer may see of the travail of his soul and be satisfied. O let the earth be speedily filled with His glory, whose Name is above every name; to whom, with thee, O Father, and thee O Holy Spirit, be ascribed, as is most due, everlasting **dominion and praise** *Amen* and *Amen*.

THE LORD'S PRAYER PARAPHRASED.

OUR Father, who art in heaven : Give us grace to draw near to thee with reverence, and to put our whole trust in thee, who art a Father always able and willing to defend and provide for thy children.—*Hallowed be thy name.* Cause us and all the world to worship thee and to serve thee acceptably, with reverence and godly fear, that **we may** sanctify thy great and glorious Name.—*Thy Kingdom come.* May all the kingdoms of this world be delivered from the tyranny of Satan, and become the kingdoms of our Lord and of his Christ. We beseech thee, O Lord, to perfect thy kingdom of grace in our souls, and to hasten thy kingdom of glory.—*Thy will be done in earth, as it is in heaven.* Grant us to know thy wise and gracious will, and to be resigned and obedient to it in all things. May thy will be done by men on earth as it is by angels in heaven, who delight to know and are always ready to do it.—*Give us this day our daily bread;* and make us content therewith. Let us not want for our bodies the meat which perisheth; nor for our souls that which endureth unto everlasting life. Daily feed our souls with the bread of life and the water of life, and help us to leave the supply of al our temporal wants to thee, who knowest what things we have need of.—*Forgive us our trespasses, as we forgive them that trespass against us.* We pray thee, for Christ's sake, to forgive us all our sins; **and to give us** grace to forgive, even as we desire to be forgiven.—*Lead us not into temptation, but deliver us from evil.* Keep us, O Lord, from temptations to sin: or support and deliver us when we are tempted. From all evil and mischief, from sin, from the crafts and assaults of the devil, from thy wrath, and from everlasting damnation, good Lord deliver us.—*For thine is the kingdom, and the power, and the glory, for ever and ever.* Thine is the kingdom, even an everlasting kingdom, a kingdom, which ruleth over all; and thy dominion endureth throughout all ages. Thou canst do what thou wilt with all thy creatures. Thine is the power, both to punish thine enemies, and to bless and defend thy people And thine is the glory of creation and redemption, and of all that thy children have, of all that they do, and of all that they hope to enjoy: for of thee, and through thee, and to thee, are all things; to whom be glory in the church, by Christ Jesus, throughout all ages, world without end. *Amen.*

THE CHILD'S FIRST PRAYER.

O LORD, make me a good child. Take care of my dear father and mother;* and my dear brothers and sisters;* keep us this day [night] from all evil and sin, and when we die take us to Heaven for Jesus Christ's sake. *Amen.*

THE CHILD'S SECOND PRAYER.

O LORD, bless me, and put thy fear and love into my heart. May I always speak the truth, and fear a lie. Bless me in my learning. May it be my delight to read thy holy word, and to do thy blessed will. Bless my dear father and mother,* and grant that I may be a comfort and a blessing to them. May I always love them, and mind what they say to me. Give them grace to train me up in the way that I should go; and may I never depart from it. Bless my dear brothers and sisters:* may we be very kind to each other, and dwell together in peace and love. Preserve and keep us this day [night] from all evil. Forgive us our sins; subdue our evil tempers, and make us holy; that, when we die, we may go to heaven, and be with Jesus Christ, our blessed Lord and Saviour. *Amen.*

Our Father, who art in Heaven, &c.

* These expressions must be varied to suit different cases.

CONCLUDING PRAYERS.

OUR Father, who art in heaven; hallowed be thy Name. Thy kingdom come. Thy will be done on earth, as it is in heaven. Give us this day our daily bread. And forgive us our trespasses, as we forgive those that trespass against us. And lead us not into temptation: But deliver us from evil. For thine is the kingdom, and the power, and the glory, for ever and ever. *Amen.*

THE grace of our Lord Jesus Christ, and the love of God, and the fellowship of the Holy Ghost, be with us all evermore. *Amen.*

GRACE, mercy, and peace, from God the Father, and from the Lord Jesus Christ our Saviour, and from the Holy Ghost the Comforter, be unto us, and all whom we should remember, now and for ever. *Amen.*

THE blessing of God Almighty, the Father, the Son, and the Holy Ghost, be upon us, and remain with us now and ever. *Amen.*

THE Lord bless us and keep us: the Lord make his face to shine upon us, and be gracious unto us; the Lord lift up his countenance upon us, and give us peace, both now and evermore. *Amen.*

GOD the Father, God the Son, God the Holy Ghost, bless, preserve, and keep us: the Lord mercifully with his favor look upon us; and so fill us with all spiritual benediction and grace, that we may so live in this life that in the world to come we may have life everlasting. *Amen.*

GRACE BEFORE MEALS.

BLESS us, O Lord, in what we are going to receive, and make us truly thankful : for Jesus Christ's sake. *Amen.*

OR :

Bless us, O Lord, in what we are going to receive; and give us grace to enjoy everything in thee, and thee in everything : through Jesus Christ. *Amen.*

OR :

With thy renewed mercies. O Lord, give us a renewed sense of thy love in them : and whether we eat, or drink, or whatsoever we do may we do all to thy glory : through Jesus Christ. *Amen.*

GRACE AFTER MEALS.

O LORD, we praise thee for all thy mercies, through Jesus Christ our Saviour. *Amen.*

OR :

Gracious God, may the food which we have received strengthen our bodies; and may thy Holy Spirit strengthen and refresh our souls : through Jesus Christ. *Amen*

OR :

Blessed Lord, as we live continually upon thy bounty, so may we always live to thy glory : through Jesus Christ. *Amen.*

The writer has been amazed and grieved at the slovenly and irreverent manner in which he has too often seen the head of a family mumble two or three words of a Grace, which, if professedly offered up to Heaven, were never likely to be accepted of that God who is to be had in reverence of all who supplicate or praise his Name. The Divine blessing should be asked, and the goodness of God acknowledged, through Jesus Christ, with an audible voice, and always in an humble, devotional frame of mind, if we would hope to enjoy the Divine favour.

A PRAYER ON ENTERING CHURCH.

POUR down upon me, O Lord, and upon this congregation, the Spirit of grace and of supplication. May we worship thee in spirit and in truth; and hear and receive thy holy word to the salvation of our souls; through Jesus Christ our Saviour. *Amen.*

A PRAYER BEFORE LEAVING CHURCH.

PARDON, O Lord, whatsoever thy pure eyes have seen amiss in me; and grant that I may not be a forgetful hearer, but a patient doer of thy word: that hereafter I may be glorified with thee for ever, through Jesus Christ our Saviour. *Amen.*

EJACULATIONS FROM SCRIPTURE.

On rising in the Morning.

I LAID me down and slept; I awaked: for the Lord sustained me. (Ps. iii. 5.)

At Noon.

Evening, and morning, and at noon, will I pray, and that instantly. (Ps. lv. 17.)

On going to Bed.

I will lay me down in peace, and take my rest; for it is thou, Lord, only, that makest me to dwell in safety (Ps. iv. 9.)

At going out

Lord, bless my going out and my coming in, from this time forth for evermore. (Ps. cxxi. 8.)

At Work.

Prosper thou the work of my hands, O Lord: prosper thou my handy-work. (Ps. xc. 17.)

In Conversation

Set a watch, O Lord, before my mouth; keep the door of my lips. (Ps. cxli. 3)

When evil-entreated.

Father, forgive them; for they know not what they do. (Luke xxiii. 34.)

Lord, lay not this sin to their charge. (Acts vii. 60.)

On any Loss.

The Lord gave, and the Lord hath taken away blessed be the name of the Lord. (Job i. 21.)

Shall we receive good at the hand of God, and shall we not receive evil? (Job ii. 10.)

In difficult Circumstances.

Cause me to know the way wherein I should walk; for I lift up my soul unto thee. (Ps. cxliii. 8.)

Lord, I am oppressed; undertake for me. (Isaiah xxxviii. 14.)

Hear, O Lord, and have mercy upon me: Lord, be thou my helper. (Ps. xxx. 10)

For a Friend.

The Lord grant unto him that he may find mercy of the Lord in that day. (2 Tim. i. 18.)

In Temptation.

How can I do this great wickedness, and sin against God? (Gen. xxxix. 9.)

Lord, cleanse thou me from secret faults: keep back thy servant also from presumptuous sins: let them not have dominion over me. (Ps. xix. 12, 13.)

Before Prayer.

Lord, teach us to pray. (Luke xi. 1.)

O Lord God of hosts, hear my prayer. Give ear O God of Jacob. (Ps. lxxxiv. 8.)

Hear me when I call, O God of my righteousness. Have mercy upon me and hear my prayer. (Ps. iv. 1.)

Before reading the Scriptures.

Open thou mine eyes that I may behold wondrous things out of thy law. (Ps. cxix. 18.)

Going to Church.

Let thy priests be clothed with righteousness, and let thy saints shout for joy. (Ps. cxxxii. 9.)

We will go into his tabernacles; we will worship at his footstool (Ps. cxxxii. 7.)

Entering the House of God.

This is none other but the house of God, and this is the gate of heaven. (Gen. xxviii. 17.)

Let the words of my mouth, and the meditation of my heart, be acceptable in thy sight, O Lord, my Strength and my Redeemer. (Ps. xix. 14.)

On hearing the Scriptures.

Sanctify us through thy truth: thy word is truth. (John xvii. 17.)

OCCASIONAL EJACULATIONS.

Arise for our help, and redeem us for thy mercies sake. (Ps. xliv. 26.)

O Lord, be gracious unto us; we have waited for thee. (Isaiah xxxiii. 2.)

Father, glorify thy name. (John xii. 28.)

Lord, save us; we perish. (Matt. viii. 25.)

Jesus, thou Son of David, have mercy on me. (Mark x. 47.)

Lord, if thou wilt, thou canst make me clean. (Luke 12.)

Lord, I believe, help thou mine unbelief. (Mark ix. 24.

HYMN I. L. M

1 WHAT various hindrances we meet
   In coming to the Mercy-seat!
Yet who, that knows the worth of prayer,
But wishes to be often there?

2 Prayer makes the darken'd cloud withdraw;
Prayer climbs the ladder Jacob saw;
Gives exercise to faith and love,
Brings every blessing from above.

3 Restraining prayer, we cease to fight;
Prayer makes the Christian's armour bright
And Satan trembles when he sees
The weakest saint upon his knees.

4 While Moses stood with arms spread wide,
Success was found on Israel's side:
But when through weariness they fail'd,
That moment Amalek prevailed.

5 Have you no words! Ah! think again:
Words flow apace when you complain,
And fill your fellow-creature's ear
With the sad tale of all your care.

6 Were half the breath thus vainly spent
To Heaven in supplication sent,
Your cheerful song would oft'ner be,
"Hear what the Lord hath done for me."

HYMN II. C M

1 LORD, teach us how to pray aright,
   With reverence and with fear:
Though dust and ashes in thy sight,
   We may, we must, draw near.

2 We perish if we cease from prayer:
   O grant us power to pray;
And, when to meet thee we prepare,
   Lord, meet us by the way.

3 Give deep humility; the sense
   Of godly sorrow give;
A strong desiring confidence
   To hear thy voice, and live.

4 Faith in the only Sacrifice
   That can for sin atone,
To cast our hopes, to fix our eyes
   On Christ, on Christ alone;

5 Patience to watch, and wait, and weep,
   Though mercy long delay;
Courage our fainting souls to keep,
   And trust Thee, though thou slay.

6 Give these—and then thy will be done:
   Thus strengthen'd with all might,
We, by thy Spirit, through thy Son,
   Shall pray, and pray aright.

HYMN III.

1 THE praying spirit breathe,
   The watching power impart;
From all entanglements beneath,
   Call off my peaceful heart.

2 My feeble mind sustain,
   By worldly thoughts oppressed;
Appear, and let me turn again
   To my eternal rest.

3 Swift to my rescue come,
   Thine own this moment seize;
Gather my wandering spirit home,
   And keep in perfect peace.

4 Suffered no more to rove
   O'er all the earth abroad,
Arrest the prisoner of thy love,
   And shut me up in God.

HYMN IV.

1 PRAYER was appointed to convey
   The blessings God designs to give;
Long as they live should Christians pray,
   For only while they pray they live.

2 And shall we in dead silence lie,
   When Christ stands waiting for our prayer!
My soul, thou hast a Friend on high—
   Arise, and try your interest there.

8 If pains afflict or wrongs oppress,
  If cares distract or fears dismay,
If guilt deject or sins distress,
  The remedy's before thee—pray.

4 'Tis prayer supports the soul that's weak,
  Though thought be broken-language lame;
Pray if thou canst or canst not speak,
  But pray with faith in Jesus' name.

HYMN V.

1 COME, my soul, thy suit prepare—
  Jesus loves to answer prayer;
  He himself has bid thee pray:
  Rise and ask without delay.

2 Thou art coming to a King—
  Large petitions with thee bring;
  For his grace and powers are such,
  None can ever ask too much.

3 With my burden I begin:
  Lord, remove this load of sin;
  Let thy blood, for sinners spilt,
  Set my conscience free from guilt

4 Lord, I come to thee for rest:
  Take possession of my breast;
  There thy blood-bought right maintain,
  And without a rival reign.

5 While I am a pilgrim here,
  Let thy love my spirit cheer;
  As my Guide, my Guard, my Friend,
  Lead me to my journey's end.

6 Show me what I have to do;
  Every hour my strength renew;
  Let me live a life of faith;
  Let me die thy people's death.

HYMN VI.

1 BEHOLD the throne of grace,
    The promise calls me near;
  There Jesus shows a smiling face,
    And waits to answer prayer.

2 That rich atoning blood,
    Which sprinkled round I see,
  Provides for those who come to God
    An all-prevailing plea.

3 My soul, ask what thou wilt—
    Thou canst not be too bold;
  Since his own blood for thee he spilt,
    What else can he withhold?
                          NEWTON.

HYMN VII.

1 JESUS, full of all compassion,
    Hear thy humble suppliant's cry;
  Let me know thy great salvation—
    See, I languish, faint, and die.

2 Guilty, but with heart relenting,
    Overwhelmed with helpless grief,
Prostrate at thy feet repenting,
    Send, oh! send me quick relief.

3 Whither should a wretch be flying
    But to Him who comfort gives?
Whither from the dread of dying
    But to Him who ever lives?

4 *Saved*, the dead shall spread new glory
    Through the shining realms above;
Angels sing the pleasing story,
    All enraptured with thy love.

HYMN VIII.

1 O THOU who wouldst not have
    One wretched sinner die,
Who died'st thyself my soul to save
    From endless misery:
Show me the way to shun
    Thy dreadful wrath severe,
That when thou comest on thy throne,
    I may with joy appear.

2 Thou art thyself the way,
    Thyself in me reveal;
So shall I spend my life's short day
    Obedient to thy will;

So shall I love my God,
  Because he first loved me.
And praise thee in thy bright abode
  To all eternity.

HYMN IX.

1 NAY, I will not let thee go
    Till a blessing thou bestow;
  Do not turn away thy face—
  Mine's an urgent, pressing case.

2. Once a sinner near despair
   Sought the mercy-seat in prayer;
   Mercy heard and set him free:
   Lord, that mercy came to me.

3 Many days have passed since then,
  Many changes I have seen,
  Yet have been upheld till now.
  Who could hold me up but thou?

4 Thou hast helped in every need—
  This emboldens me to plead;
  After so much mercy past,
  Canst thou let me sink at last?

5 No, I must maintain my hold—
  This thy goodness makes me bold;
  I can no denial take,
  Since I plead for Jesus' sake.

HYMN X.   L. M.

1 MY hope, my all, my Saviour thou!
    To thee, lo, now my soul I bow;
I feel the bliss thy wounds impart;
I find thee, Saviour, in my heart.

2 Be thou my strength, be thou my way;
Protect me through my life's short day;
In all my acts may wisdom guide,
And keep me, Saviour, near thy side.

3 Correct, reprove, and comfort me;
As I have need, my Saviour be;
And if I would from thee depart,
Then clasp me, Saviour, to thy heart.

4 In fierce temptation's darkest hour,
Save me from sin and Satan's power;
Tear every idol from thy throne,
And reign, my Saviour, reign alone.

5 My suff'ring time shall soon be o'er,
Then shall I sigh and weep no more;
My ransom'd soul shall soar away,
To sing thy praise in endless day.

HYMN XI.   L. M

1 O JESUS, let thy dying cry
    Pierce to the bottom of my heart;
Its evils cure, its wants supply,
    And bid my unbelief depart!

2 Slay the dire root and seed of sin;
   Prepare for thee the holiest place;
Then, O essential Love! come in,
   And fill thy house with endless praise.

3 Let me, according to thy word,
   A tender, contrite heart receive,
Which grieves at having grieved its Lord,
   And never can itself forgive:

4 A heart thy joys and griefs to feel:
   A heart that cannot faithless prove:
A heart where Christ alone my dwell,
   All praise, all meekness, and all love.

HYMN XII.   S. M

1 IN true and patient hope,
   My soul, on God attend;
And calmly, confidently look
   Till he salvation send.

2 I shall his goodness see,
   While on his name I call;
He will defend and strengthen me,
   And I shall never fall.

3 Jesus, to thee I fly,
   My refuge and my tower;
Upon thy faithful love rely,
   And find thy saving power.

HYMN XIII.   C. M.

1 FATHER, I stretch my hands to thee—
    No other help I know;
If thou withdraw thyself from me,
    Ah! whither shall I go?

2 What did thine only Son endure,
    Before I drew my breath!
What pain, what labor, to secure
    My soul from endless death!

3 O Jesus, could I this believe,
    I now should feel thy power;
Now my poor soul thou wouldst retrieve,
    Nor let me wait one hour.

4 Author of faith, to thee I lift
    My weary, longing eyes:
Oh! let me now receive that **gift**—
    My soul without it dies.

5 Surely thou canst not let me die;
    Oh! speak, and I shall live;
And here I will unwearied lie,
    Till thou thy Spirit give.

6 The worst of sinners would rejoice,
    Could they but see thy face:
Oh! let me hear thy quick'ning voice,
    And taste thy pardoning grace!

HYMN XIV.

1 DEPTH of mercy, can there be
    Mercy still reserved for me?
  Can my God his wrath forbear?
  Me, the chief of sinners, spare?

2 I have long withstood his grace,
  Long provok'd him to his face;
  Would not hearken to his calls,
  Grieved him by a thousand falls.

3 Kindled his relentings are—
  Me he now delights to spare;
  Cries, "How shall I give thee up?"
  Lets the lifted thunder drop.

4 There for me the Saviour stands,
  Shows his wounds, and spreads his **hands**
  God is love! I know, I feel,
  Jesus weeps and loves me still.

5 Jesus, answer from above—
  Is not all thy nature love?
  Wilt thou then the wrong **forget?**
  Suffer me to kiss thy feet?

6 Now incline me to repent!
  Let me now my fall lament!
  Now my foul revolt deplore,
  Weep, believe, and sin no **more.**

WESLEY.

HYMN XV.   L M

1 O GOD, most merciful and true,
   Thy nature to my soul impart;
'Stablish with me the cov'nant new,
   And stamp thine image on my heart.

2 To real holiness restored,
   Oh! let me gain my Saviour's mind,
And in the knowledge of my Lord,
   Fulness of life eternal find.

3 Remember, Lord, my sins no more,
   That them I may no more forget,
But, sunk in guiltless shame, adore
   With speechless wonder at thy feet.

4 O'erwhelm'd with thy stupendous grace,
   I shall not in thy presence move,
But breathe unutterable praise,
   And rapturous awe, and silent love.

5 Then every murmuring thought and vain,
   Expires, in sweet confusion lost;
I cannot of my cross complain,
   I cannot of my goodness boast.

6 Pardon'd for all that I have done,
   My mouth as in the dust I hide;
And glory give to God alone,
   My God for ever pacified.

HYMN XVI. C. M.

Salvation by the Blood of the Lamb.

1 THERE is a fountain filled with blood,
　　Drawn from Immanuel's veins:
And sinners plunged beneath that flood.
　　Lose all their guilty stains.

2 The dying thief rejoiced to see
　　That fountain in his day,
And there may I, though vile as he,
　　Wash all my sins away.

3 Dear dying Lamb, thy precious blood
　　Shall never lose its power,
Till all the ransomed church of God
　　Be saved, to sin no more.

4 E'er since by faith I saw the stream
　　Thy flowing wounds supply,
Redeeming love has been my theme,
　　And shall be till I die.

5 Then, in a nobler, sweeter song,
　　I'll sing thy power to save,
When this poor lisping, stammering tongue
　　Lies silent in the grave.

www.ingramcontent.com/pod-product-compliance
Lightning Source LLC
Chambersburg PA
CBHW031606110426
42742CB00037B/1302